Testaments
of Faith

But I am like a green olive tree
in the house of God . . .

Psalm 52:8

Testaments of Faith by Roy Z. Kemp

Published by The C. R. Gibson Company

This book is dedicated

with love and affection

to my niece,

Carolyn Sutphin Jenkins

Copyright © MCMLXX by
The C. R. Gibson Company, Norwalk, Connecticut
All rights reserved
Printed in the United States of America
Library of Congress Catalog Card Number: 76-91820
SBN 8378-1784-6

Contents

Love

"God is love."

I John 4:8

Love

The great commandment preached by Jesus Christ was that we love God and one another. This is very hard for some people to comprehend. But each person has within him the power to love, although often he is either unwilling to express this love or is unaware of the power that is his. In order that this great commandment be followed, it is necessary that we have the will to love.

The answer of Jesus Christ to all of us in this chaotic world of strife and suffering, fear and doubt, desperation, dissatisfaction and discontent, is simply and clearly this one thing: "Thou shalt love thy neighbour as thyself." Mark 12:31.

When a person has love, he has everything that is worthwhile. Without love, he is nothing; he has nothing. But love of God and of man must never be an empty sentiment. Love must be put into practice; it must be an inherent part of our lives. We must be concerned with other people.

We must never be guilty of indifference for the plight of others, nor stand aloof when there is a need for the help that we can give. We must feel and know compassion, and be sensitive to the needs of others. One who loves much is forgiven much. Callousness of heart is one of the deadly sins.

There is a certain spiritual dimension in any interest that we may have in the welfare of others, whether our concern is shown on the active or the contemplative level. Love, in the language of our Lord Jesus Christ, is not only a thirst, it is an overwhelming yearning.

Our love should not be kept in reserve for a few special people whom we like. But just as God's blessings fall upon everyone — the just and the unjust so we must let our love flow freely to every member of the human race. "God is no respecter of persons." Acts 10:34. We, as sons of God, must follow His example, without judgment, without first waiting for any demonstration of love to be shown to us, and without expectation of a measured return for our efforts.

One of the greatest things that will help us to love other people is to have great enthusiasm. An enthusiastic person is a lovable person, and he is able to transmit love by enthusiastic measures. He is filled with life, excitement, zest, happiness, and his enthusiasm becomes contagious. Barriers can be broken, prejudices and bias can be discarded, hatred can be done away with, when enthusiasm takes over.

"Let us love one another: for love is of God; and every one that loveth is born of God, and knoweth God. He that loveth not, knoweth not God; for God is love." I John 4:7-8.

"Let us not love in word, neither in tongue; but in deed and in truth." I John 3:18.

"Love worketh no ill to his neighbour: therefore love is the fulfilling of the law." Romans 13:10.

The prophet Micah sets forth a threefold pattern of conduct that is pleasing to God: justice, mercy, humility. "He hath shewed thee, O man, what is good; and what doth the Lord require of thee, but to do justly, and to love mercy, and to walk humbly with thy God?" Micah 6:8.

The Christian will find in this message the motivation for the good life, and a measure to follow in showing love for his neighbor.

The principles of morality do not change, nor do they vary

10

with popular fancy. The Christian will do justice in conformity with God's revealed will; he will love and show mercy because God is loving and merciful; and he will walk humbly with his God for this is a mark of Christian discipleship.

He is deeply aware that the way of humility is the way to spiritual greatness.

The brotherhood of man is a noble concept, but it takes on meaning only when it is identified with our being sons of God. Those who would walk the pathway that leads to eternal life must find a mutual love one for another by a common faith in the Lord Jesus Christ. It is only when we find our relationship with Him that we shall surely walk the pathway of righteousness.

"Can two walk together, except that they be agreed?" Amos 3:3. Christian love for someone does not always mean that we must like him. Christian love has been defined as "love of the unlovable" or the "love of the unloved."

"Ye have heard that it hath been said, Thou shalt love thy neighbour, and hate thine enemy. But I say unto you, Love your enemies, bless them that curse you, do good to them that hate you, and pray for them which despitefully use you, and persecute you; That ye may be the children of your Father which is in heaven: for he maketh his sun to rise on the evil and on the good, and sendeth rain on the just and the unjust. For if ye love them which love you, what reward have ye? do not even the publicans the same?" Matthew 5:43-46.

Service of love performed in the name of our blessed Saviour will not go unrewarded. The diligent practice of Christian benevolence will bring genuine satisfaction. And we, as children of God, must consider it a glorious privilege to assist others who are less fortunate than we.

11

In Ephesians 4:32, we are admonished: "Be ye kind one to another, tenderhearted, forgiving one another, even as God for Christ's sake hath forgiven you."

It is a sign of growth in grace when we find more joy in giving than in receiving. "It is more blessed to give than to receive." Acts 20:35.

Matthew 10:42 states: "And whosoever shall give to drink unto one of these little ones a cup of cold water only in the name of a disciple, verily I say unto you, he shall in no wise lose his reward."

We should never become weary in well-doing and in obeying the Master's command. Our deeds may seem small and insignificant to us and even to others, but they will loom large in the eyes of God when they are done in His name and with a heart overflowing with love for Him.

Heart's Doorway

Live not within the prison of yourself,
This small world turns spirit into clod.
The more ingrown the self-preoccupation,
The less room left for others and for God.

A self-obsession leads to spirit's bondage.
We must love God and all our fellowmen;
Heart's doorway must be opened wide in friendship
Where both the foe and friend are welcomed in.

Inside God's Hands

Creator of the sky and earth and stars,
The firmament and every living thing,
God's presence knows no boundaries or bars,
And all of heaven's angels gladly sing
To feel Him near. And yet, inside His hands
Which made all things, is room for you and me.
How close He is! How well He understands.
God's love will cover all abundantly.

Sharing God's Love

If words were able to express
The things the heart can hold,
The faith and hope and peace I know
Could easily be told.

But since speech is so limited
And words cannot impart
The greatness of God's love within,
I'll try to share each part.

Prayer for Service

God, give me strength to aid the maim and weak;
Give me the eyes to help the halt and blind;
Grant me the speech for those who cannot speak;
Lord, give to me an understanding mind.

I do not ask for glory nor for fame
Nor any adulation. Give to me
The power to sing and praise Thy holy name.
Let me grow ever closer, Lord, to Thee.

Speak Through Me!

Lord, may some little word of mine
    So brightly shine
Into another's darkened hour
    Its magic power
Will give him strength to go his way
    Another day.

Lord, let my feeble offering
    Cause heart to sing
And eyes to brighten. Let Thy word
    That he has heard
Be passed along to other ears;
    Bless each that hears.

14

God's Love

The love of God — it glorifies,
It makes my spirit free,
No greater love nor greater gift
Was ever given me.

God's love inspires, it gives me hope,
Makes faith grow stronger still,
And in its all redemptive grace,
I'll better do His will.

The love of God — so great, complete,
Incomprehensible encompassing full,
Is love divine, abounding love
That is immeasurable.

Vulnerability

A man may wind about his heart
A cord of steel, to fence it in,
To keep it dark, alone, apart
From stranger and from kith and kin.

But love and friendship have a way
Of breaking through a barricade,
To let the golden light of day
Shine in and strengthen one afraid.

15

God's Gifts

God gave a lily purity.
> Its chaste, white beauty He bestows
> To show no greater beauty grows,
No greater loveliness to see.

A rippling field of ripened wheat,
> More golden than the goldenrod,
> Reveals the kindly heart of God.
He lets it grow that man may eat.

Little Things

A friendly smile will always bring
A joy to others. And a word
Of praise and admiration brings
New life to someone who has heard.

The things which count are little things,
And these are needed most of all.
Great things may come of little things;
No service, in itself, is small.

Belief

*"Having the same spirit of faith....
I believed."*

II Corinthians 4:13

Belief

The power of belief is tremendous, one of life's most dynamic forces. Belief is absolutely necessary for any endeavor. The greatest factor in any undertaking is one's belief in it.

Belief can bring the impossible into the realm of the possible, if such is God's will. The ninth chapter of the Gospel of St. Mark vividly illustrates that the things which are impossible for man are possible with God, if there is belief on the part of man. In Verse 23, Jesus informs us: "If thou canst believe, all things are possible to him that believeth."

Belief and faith will enable everyone to receive the fullness of life. The amazing power of belief is that it enables us to overcome difficulties and to reach our goal. When belief contains the love of Jesus Christ our blessed Saviour, there will never be any disillusionment nor failure in our undertakings. Belief will bring victory to us.

Every person in this world who has accomplished great things, has been a great believer. Every man who possesses a love of God and has faith and belief, is master of himself. He is a person who makes a dedicated effort in his every undertaking. He has envisioned his goal. He has confidence; anticipates success.

Many find it difficult to believe unless absolute proof is shown to them. These are the "Doubting Thomases." Thomas, a disciple of Jesus, refused to believe the other disciples when they told him that the Lord Jesus was alive. Thomas believed only when Jesus appeared before him in person.

19

The spirit of the living God motivated the Saviour of mankind, and today His spirit lives. It carries on through the lives of all who have discovered the true purpose of life and pooled their resources with His. With Emerson, each of these may say: "All I have seen teaches me to trust the Creator for all that I have not seen."

Everyone carries within his heart some expectation of being able to fulfill cherished plans. We keep alive such expressions as "While there's life, there's hope"; "Hope springs eternal in the human breast"; and "Let's hope for the best."

This expectation of good from God can bring comfort and peace, for God is the source of all good. His image and likeness is spiritual and perfect, the expression of infinite goodness. Each one of us is able to develop our spiritual sense — our consciousness of the ever-presence of good — to the point where our hopes are fulfilled, and we see evidence on every side that good alone is real.

Belief is our answer to God's knocking at the door of our heart, seeking to make Himself known. To believe in God is to believe in reason. Both reasoning ability and faith are gifts of God. A living faith depends upon what we believe about Christ, the Son of God.

His life will begin when faith and belief begin. But with a light of hope in his eyes, a fire of inspiration on his tongue and lips, a love in his heart and with belief instilled in his soul, mind and heart, man will experience a radiant, majestic glory.

God's reality must be believed and accepted. There is no other proof than one's own heart. Faith is not blind credulity, but one's heart and mind can accept God without questioning, without doubting. When we come to Christ Jesus, we begin to find a real purpose to life. Only then does life begin in

earnest for us. And when the Son of God steps into our lives, there can be no conflict of interests.

God does not explain things to us nor inform us of His ways. We must trust Him and believe that He knows what is best for us. We must stop asking "Why?" and, instead, ask "How?" How can we be used by God and man for Christian witnesses, for His glory?

All those who believe in God's own Son and have received Him into their hearts, are called the children of God. This faith — this belief — is created in us by the Holy Spirit. We are become new creatures in Christ and His atoning cross, and we must bear witness to Him in this fast-changing world. "The just shall live by faith." Romans 1:17.

When we actually believe, we accept as a fact that Jesus Christ is the Good News of our salvation, and that God has spoken to us through His Son. Jesus died for our sins and He lives to bring us everlasting life. Therefore, we should believe in Him as a fact of our redemption. We must speak of what we believe in the formal creeds of our church, in our personal testimony and in the actions of our lives.

"We having the same spirit of faith, according as it is written, I believed, and therefore have I spoken; we also believe, and therefore speak." 2 Corinthians 4:13.

"My mouth shall speak the praise of the Lord: and let all flesh bless his holy name for ever and ever." Psalm 145:21.

The Holy Spirit has His most effective workers and servants in those convinced Christians who willingly tell in their own words and by their actions what Jesus Christ means to them.

But we must strive for a greater eloquence in Christian living. People need words also; good deeds are never enough, in themselves. "Faith cometh by hearing, and hearing by the

21

word of God." Romans 10:17. Paul, in Romans 1:16, says "For I am not ashamed of the gospel of Christ: for it is the power of God unto salvation to every one that believeth."

This power of God's Word is the means by which He sows the seeds of faith and belief in our hearts. And in Isaiah 40:8, we read: "The word of our God shall stand for ever."

Through belief in the blessed Saviour, Jesus Christ, the guilt of sin is removed from our hearts and the fears of judgment to come are gone. The new morning of faith brings the opportunity for a consecrated life of service to our Lord, and the glorious hope of our eternal salvation.

Healing Power

One should not be amazed to find that grief
And pain and sorrow can bring strange release,
If bravely borne. A strength beyond belief
Each one will give; each gives a healing peace.

Each one can bless and comfort those who mourn,
Whose hearts are filled with ache and bitter sorrow,
Whose souls are anguished and whose lives are torn.
And each will help to bring a bright tomorrow.

God often moves in a mysterious way
To bring His peace to hearts, to dry the tears
Of eyes that hurt. One finds that sorrow's day
Brings strength to live for coming happy years.

22

Belief

I did not see the cruel cross
Nor crown of thorns He wore,
And yet I know Christ died for me
And all my sins He bore.

I did not see the sealed tomb
Nor hear those ones who cried;
I was not there, and yet I know
Upon the cross Christ died.

Yet I believe that Christ still lives!
His love is still a part
Of every soul that will believe.
He lives within my heart.

Conviction

My life seems empty as can be
And there seems nothing left for me,
Yet — something in me still remains:
My heart a little hope retains.

Life can be lived if there is hope,
If hands still search and seek and grope.
I'll hold my heart an empty cup,
And know that God will fill it up.

House of the Lord

To live in the house of the Lord and God,
Your heart must forgive and forget;
For it is a house that perfection has made
And is free and is clear of all debt.

No jealousy lives in the house of the Lord,
No littleness, meanness, nor pain;
Contentment and happiness, joy that is sweet,
Are the tenants, and beauty does reign.

Our God is the Host, and He beckons us in.
And His love is a bond none can sever.
Each person should enter and live in its peace,
Be guests of the God-Host forever.

Weapons

Doubt will bring a proud man low,
    Dread will kill his dream,
Fear will never let him know
    Another man's esteem.

Courage will instill his heart
    With power, great and strong,
And confidence will not depart
    When heart is full of song.

The Inner Glow

The candle of the Lord should shine
    Within your heart, and glow,
No matter what the circumstance,
    No matter where you go.

The precious shining radiance
    Will brightly light within
If God's great love abides with you
    And shelters you from sin.

A radiant personality,
    A glowing of the face
Result from closer talks with God
    Within a secret place.

Courageousness

He who knows doubt will have no great tomorrow,
His dream is small, his heart knows dread and fear.
His future will be filled with pain and sorrow;
There is no brightness in his coming year.

But he who looks with great anticipation,
With eagerness for what the future brings,
Possesses courage, knows a great elation,
And has a heart which gaily, proudly sings.

Searchers

One climbed the highest mountain peak
    And stood on toes to reach in space,
A closeness to his God to seek,
    To look upon His holy face.
Yet emptiness was all he found —
He did not stand on holy ground.

Another sought to reach his God,
    But quietly knelt down to pray.
There on his knees in lowly sod,
    He knew to be the only way
To see his God, — in humble prayer.
He found that God was standing there.

Valueness

A faith that has not known a great fulfillment;
A love that lives alone with no word spoken;
A back that shows no searing scars of lashes;
A dream that has not had its edges broken;
A breast that has not bared itself to flame;
A heart that has not known achievement's fever;
A hope that has not ever tried to live;
A loom that does not have a skillful weaver.

26

Worship

"O come, let us worship."

Psalm 95:6

Worship

Worship is a conscious effort to know God and to draw closer to Him. When we seek God, we worship. We should make our worship a definite part of every day. The busier our life, the greater the need for contact with God. After worship, we have a surer sense of values, a clear vision of purpose and a better defined perspective.

We can experience worship within the doors of His church, under His great open spaces, beneath His trees or in the quietness of our own homes.

"God is a Spirit: and they that worship him must worship him in spirit and in truth." John 4:24.

God makes it clear through the prophet Hosea that He is not satisfied with the mere external forms of worship. "For I desired mercy, and not sacrifice; and the knowledge of God more than burnt offerings." Hosea 6:6.

To worship God in the right manner, we must know Him. We must not just acknowledge His existence by recalling certain Biblical facts. In doing only this, we are just knowing Him with our minds. True worship of God means the intimacy of faith and fellowship with His Son, Jesus Christ — total commitment to His cause.

In this way, we shall display the "mercy" which God desires. If we truly know Him in our heart, we shall reflect His Spirit in our daily life. Thus our whole life will be a true worship of God; we will follow His commandments and be dwellers in His church.

God's church is one and indivisible. It is neither limited nor divided by time or space. It includes all true believers in Christ — both those who now live in Him and those who have died in Him, since the world's beginning.

"The saints on earth and those above but one communion make," we sing, and the hymn goes on to say: "One family, we dwell in Him, One church above, beneath, though now divided by the stream, the narrow stream, of death."

It should give us all reassurance that our loved ones who have gone before us in the Lord have not been removed from our fellowship, but still share with us the same blessed communion. Theirs is the glorious prize, ours is the happy prospect. The day will come when we shall join with them before the heavenly throne, and that will be a joyous reunion, indeed.

Prayer is a request for divine cooperation. Faith and learning are the hope of the future and the light of the world.

"For he is thy Lord; and worship thou him." Psalm 45:11.

"O come, let us worship and bow down: let us kneel before the Lord our maker." Psalm 95:6.

The solution to economic and social injustice lies only in the high ideals and the serious application of the Christian gospel. That gospel directs us to "an house not made with hands, eternal in the heavens." 2 Corinthians 5:1.

We make our peace with God through the Cross, where Christ shed His blood for our sins, and it is only through Christ that we can find true joy, peace, contentment and eternal salvation for our soul.

The most important thing in our worship of God is our true sincerity. Worship must never be a false thing. Such worship is hypocrisy. Empty ceremony of worship reveals only an empty life, one completely without purpose.

30

In Haggai 2:9, we read: "The glory of this latter house shall be greater than of the former, saith the Lord of hosts: and in this place will I give peace."

In this stirring prophecy, Haggai speaks of the church in the New Testament era. Christ has come to establish His church among men. The church is His spiritual body, of which He is the head and His people are the members. His church is eternal, universal, holy. Its membership includes all those who accept Jesus Christ as their Saviour, in faith, and in life. It is found wherever the Gospel is preached. It is the communion of saints.

It is through the church, through the ministry of the Word and the sacraments, that God makes known His glory to us. Within the church's strong embrace we are brought into communion with our Lord and behold the beauty of His grace.

To receive a feeling of joy and victory, we must feel deeply the glory of life and of things to come. There must be a new expectation. We must walk with anticipation, with newness of spirit. We must feel the surging upthrust of belief, confidence, faith. We must gain an optimistic outlook and walk with gladness and lightness.

Optimism expresses hope and newness. It is a philosophy based on the belief that basically life is good, created and sustained by a good and loving God, and that in the long run of life, the good over-balances the evil.

The poet Walt Whitman wrote: "To me, every hour of the light and dark is a miracle."

The person who practices optimism, finds joy.

31

Plea for Mercy

Oh, God, we know Thy patience
    Is wonderful and great.
How long shall it continue?
    How long, God, will Thou wait
For all the errant pilgrims
    To heed unto Thy call?
Lord, be Thou patient longer
    And do not cause the Fall!

Their way is rough and rugged
    And hurtful to their feet;
They cannot see Thy way is clear,
    Is fragrant, fresh and sweet.
Lord, give them greater wisdom
    And make each pilgrim see
The way to full obedience,
    The only way to Thee.

Waves of Influence

A pebble tossed into a lake
    Sinks to the depths below,
But it creates small waves which reach
    Far as the lake can go.

So can the Word of God, received
In hearts which have a lack,
Make forceful waves which reach
To the end of the world and back.

The Power of Christ

Christ can still the storms of fear,
uncertainty and doubt
And give to you an inner peace and
bring to you new rest.
He'll bear your load of weariness and
give you strength to shout
For joy and rapture; He will give
to you new thankfulness.

Christ puts new vision in your eyes,
your mind, and in your heart.
He clears your way to better things —
serenity of soul,
New confidence and hope and faith;
showers of blessings start.
For Christ will cleanse away your sin,
will make you pure and whole.

33

Willing Laborer

I truly have a need of God
    And God has need of me,
And I shall strive to do His will,
    To live obediently.

God knows my needs. He will supply;
    His service never fails.
And on His mission I shall go,
    No matter what prevails.

A time misspent is wasted time.
    I'll race and shall not plod;
Each moment doing not God's work
    Is to deny my God.

Incompleteness

A loaf is only half a loaf
Unless the loaf we share;
The best of teaching is a waste
On one who does not care;
The strongest faith is but a sham,
As useless as a clod,
Unless the heart sings songs of joy
And praise unto its God.

The Quest

While all the world's religions
    Record man's futile quest
To find God and to know Him,
    And thus find peace and rest,
Christianity must teach us
    That God comes down to man;
He seeks the errant pilgrim
    In every way He can.

Inner Search

I searched for God, but when I found
That all was arid, barren ground,
I stopped my search — sat down and cried,
Then found Him standing by my side.

When eyes are used to search for God,
They're no more useful than a clod.
To find Him when we're far apart,
Search must be made with mind and heart.

Homebound Pilgrims

There are the low, dark moments
When hearts plod through the dust,
When faith and hope have weakened
And faint has grown our trust.
We walk with eyes cast downward,
And darkness reigns within
When heart and mind are tested
And doubt and fear begin.

But high exhilaration
Will come again some day
If we have faith and trust
To walk God's chosen way.
God's outstretched hands will guide us,
Not one of us shall fall
If we, His homebound pilgrims,
Will only heed His call.

The Opened Door

To many, it seems foolishness
    To preach Christ crucified,
Yet God would have this message preached,
    For on the cross Christ died.

And it is comforting to know
　　(We should have known before).
In faith, we have access to God;
　　Faith is the opened door.

Helpfulness

When we share
The things we treasure,
Blessings come
In heaping measure,
Then our hearts
Will grow much lighter
For each day
Will be much brighter.

When we smile
And do a kindness,
Heart has vision
And not blindness.
When we strive
To fill a need,
Heart will feel
Great peace, indeed.

What Man Must Learn

There are external lessons man must learn,
Inspiring truths by which he must abide;
And basic things which feed a hungry soul,
Be recognized and deeply felt inside.

In every heart there is an urgent need
To find a haven from each dangerous storm;
In each of us, there is a perfect mold
By which our character is given form.

The freedom which can loose the iron chains
Of prejudice, intolerance, and hate
Must be experienced by every man
Who would achieve an honorable estate.

Each one of us is different and unique
Yet each of us was born to be God's child
In each of us there is a spark divine
Each one of us will know His mercy mild.

Humility

"Humble yourselves."

I Peter 5:6

Humility

Humility is the most needed virtue of the Christian. Jesus spoke of this in His sermon on the Mount, when He said, "Blessed are the poor in spirit for theirs is the kingdom of heaven." Matthew 5:3.

Again we are told, in Luke 18:14: "For every one that exalteth himself shall be abased, but he that humbleth himself shall be exalted."

In I Peter 5:6, we read: "Humble yourselves therefore under the mighty hand of God, that He may exalt you in due time."

Kindness should be reflected in all that we do or say. Man's biggest problem is man himself. Man is selfish and self-centered by his very nature. We see this in the nations of the world as well as in ourselves and in others. When a person is more interested in what he wants than in what God wants, or when he puts himself first and God second, he is committing a sin.

In Matthew 16:24, Jesus informs us: "If any man will come after me, let him deny himself, and take up his cross, and follow me."

Jesus asks that we follow Him, regardless of the self-denial and the sacrifice that this may require. And if we love Him as He loves us, then we shall go wherever He leads, willingly and faithfully. He obtained forgiveness for our selfishness by His death on the cross for us.

Man is a proud creature, proud of his accomplishments

and achievements. And yet, man does not own anything. He owes everything to the God who made him and who supplies his every need. He came into this world with nothing, and he will leave this world with nothing. All that he is, all that he has, is given him by God, his Maker. His life should, therefore, be one continuous "Thank you, God!" for all his many blessings.

Man is egotistical, but he may begin to regard pride and humility in a different light when his perspective becomes free of false standards. There is something in humility which lifts the heart.

To be devout, one must first become humble, for devotion is the application of an humble heart to service and love for God.

In the providence of a living God, the still small voice may be heard above the gale forces of our time. Meekness and humility have been misunderstood and misrepresented. Properly presented, they are essential Christian virtues. Neither is to be associated with weak compliance, listless acceptance of things, nor are they to be considered the doormat philosophies of life.

Neither of these qualities in a person is any reason for him to become weak and spineless. Rather than being accepted as synonymous with weakness of character, these qualities should be recognized as being channelled and directed energies whose source and being are conscious and loving obedience to the will of God.

Neither meekness nor humility should ever permit a person to lose the capacity for indignation in the presence of evil and sin. Rather, they are the very qualities which should enable him to retain his clear reasoning and his capacity to

42

deal with harshness and injustice without resorting to retaliation through anger and provocation.

Meekness and humility will not spare a person from adversity, loss, hardships and injustice or from any of the other evils of life, but they will give to him the strength, courage and understanding to triumph over these things.

The person with humility considers himself to be a simple child of God, and there is deeply embedded in his being the knowledge that "with God all things are possible." Matthew 19:26.

Meekness and humility indicate a way of life. They will conquer evil with good, for each is a special spiritual discipline. Their possessors will know a kind of childlike faith in God.

Ways of Life

Who lives a life of godlessness,
One filled with greed and waste,
One filled with hate and prejudice,
Of bitterness will taste.

But he who knows a love for God,
Does good from day to day,
Will know life's sweetness, for he lives
God's own appointed way.

"A Certain Samaritan"

These three brief words present to view
Descriptively one of the few
Men of compassion we may know,
Upon the road to Jericho.

Enough is told that we may see
An act that lives eternally;
A glorious and shining deed
That met and filled a human need.

We are not told the Samaritan's name.
There was no need. Love brought him fame.
Lord, may we, too, by love and grace,
Perform Thy work and win our place.

Rarity

We need to walk God's chosen way
    And let His Spirit lead,
For if we'll only follow Him,
    He'll fill our every need.
It does not take a prophet nor
    A wise man nor a seer
To realize God's way of life
    Is one we must hold dear.

We need to pray soul-searchingly,
   To talk with God's dear Son,
To feel His presence, asking that
   His will, not ours, be done.
And rare it is at all to find,
   No matter where we seek,
A soul that's silent, quiet, still
   Enough to hear God speak!

Fame

Our fame may come from some small deed of kindness.
Fame is not born alone of courage, skill,
Or of great strength. Who helps a needful neighbor,
Performs a worthy work; such action will
Be long remembered; for a helping hand,
When badly needed, fits into God's plan.
The Bible speaks of such a worthy person
And labels him a "Good Samaritan."

An act of service which is long remembered
And honored by the memory, is fame,
Although the person who may give the service
May go his way and never give his name.
Courageous is the man who does his part
Although it may not be a daring deed,
And fame will honor him. He was a man
Who proved himself by following his creed.

Charitable Heart

True peace is known, a joy supreme,
    A life is doubly blest,
When justice plays a major part
    In any person's breast.

For true contentment will reside
    And happiness will reign
When charity lives in his heart
    And mercy has domain.

Permanence in Sand

Men write their messages on scrolls,
    Engrave in granite regal creeds,
Emblazon on their parchment rolls
    Telling all their wondrous deeds.

But One who came with mighty power
    And walked quite humbly through the land,
Served man for His allotted hour,
    And wrote His message in the sand.

The words are unrecorded now,
    The words He pencilled in the sand,
And yet, in every heart, somehow,
    They live and help heart understand.

46

The books and charts will be discarded,
    The spoken voice not long be heard,
Yet these shall always be regarded:
    Each slowly pencilled, vivid word.

Understanding

It is wise to make allowance
For another person's fault,
To forgive a small shortcoming
And to never give assault
To his pride or to his thinking,
Though you think you really must;
Do not give him condemnation
But, instead, show him your trust.

Help him be more understanding
Of the problems you must face;
Furnish him the aid and guidance
Which will help him to erase
Any error in his thinking,
Change his reason and his plan;
With your guidance, he'll develop
Into a much better man.

Moral Fibre

God never meant that we should run
    In cowardice, with fears,
With trembling knee and quaking heart,
    When any danger nears.

He gave us courage, faith and hope,
    The strength to stand our ground
And fight for justice, truth and right
    Where these cannot be found.

Silent Praise

I know God loves tranquillity.
He loves a peacefulness in hearts.
His seasons move and make no sound
As one comes in and one departs.

And silently the hours pass,
The moments and the minutes run
In silence, and no sound is made
By God's magnificent bright sun.

His moon, with stillness, peacefully,
Rules over night's cloud-studded sky.
And all God's twinklng stars at night
Are hushed and still and mute and shy.

So we, His children, must be mute
And let our hearts be still and calm;
To worship God with silent praise
Can be a healing, soothing balm.

A Word of Scandal

A quick, hot fire,
A vivid flame
Whose purpose is
To ruin a name,
Is started by
One single word,
One silent whisper
Faintly heard.

Lips, be careful
And discreet!
Ears may hear
And mouths repeat
Your spoken word.
Tongues, be still!
One single word
Can maim and kill.

Values

In hearts that know a love for God
    Are values we should know;
They fill the heart with radiance
    And leave a shining glow.

These values, which are mercy, truth
    And justice, kindness, love
And charity and reverence,
    Are given by God above.

Prayer For Help

Father, place Thy hand in mine
For now I am afraid
To walk the byways and the roads
Of a world I never made.

Look down with mercy and with love
Upon those here who grope
In darkness and despair, to find
Some small bright gleam of hope.

Lord, send us courage, give us strength,
Be merciful to us
Until Thy blessed Son returns
To reign victorious.

50

Grief

"And when he was come near, he beheld the city, and wept over it."

Luke 19:41

Grief

A strong faith and a deep personal Christian conviction are not composed of stoicism. It is only natural for us to grieve over the loss of someone very close to us or of something that is very important to us.

Grieving is a natural part of living. There is a time for grief in everyone's life. It is something which cannot be avoided, for it is inevitable. Grief is a natural part of human experience.

Grief can be the fire which will strengthen our basic qualities of understanding, sympathy, gentleness and kindness. If we can learn to maintain our close relationship with God through our period of grief, we will find that our faith has been strengthened and increased by our ordeal.

The Scriptures tell us in many places that the strong and hard men of old often wept bitterly. Their tears were with them often. One of the strongest and most vivid and heart-rending verses in the Bible is, "Jesus wept." John 11:35.

In Luke 19:41, we read: "And when he was come near, he beheld the city, and wept over it."

The Psalmist sings to us: "For his anger endureth but a moment; in his favor is life: weeping may endure for a night, but joy cometh in the morning." Psalm 30:5.

Our Lord Jesus experienced feelings of loneliness, sorrow, and of having been forsaken and left alone with His great sorrows and griefs. His cry on the cross, "My God, my God, why hast thou forsaken me?" Mark 15:34 is the most poignant passage in the Scripture.

53

Grief can create a great change within us. We can come out of the experience stronger and better, or we can allow the experience to weaken us, mentally, morally and spiritually. But grief should never be so great that it restrains us from recovery.

Faith will help us recover. Trust in Christ and in God's great justice will sustain us in our hour of need. It will enable us to return to our normal way of life when it is the proper time to do so. Spiritual and emotional maturity will create an inner strength and tranquility, which will enable us to see and know that God still reigns, the sun still shines, the flowers still bloom and the birds still sing, despite our personal sorrow and tragedy.

Usually, after a deep grief, there will come a time of depression when our future looks dark, our thinking uncertain and vague and our thoughts unsure. This is a trying period of doubt, fear, loneliness and uncertainty.

This is the period in our lives when true friendship means the most to us. A grieving person needs companionship and sympathy. But these needs must be met with tact and diplomacy; not everyone reacts in the same manner.

Often, when a deep grief comes to us, our initial experience is a feeling of shock and of unbelief. We just cannot under-stand or comprehend that it has actually occurred. In a sense, this is a good thing because it is a temporary anesthesia, which allows our physical and mental capacities to absorb the shock gradually.

But this feeling of numbed disbelief should not remain for too long a period. The sooner one can return to his normal way of life after experiencing a great and upsetting shock from grief, the better it will be for him. There is therapeutic

54

value in a returning as soon as possible to one's regular mode of living.

Deep, personal grief should not be a time to wallow in gloom and depression. Each thing should be given its proper place in our lives. Recovery from grief should be a natural occurrence. We can continue to be happy and to know great joy, even though we have experienced the fiery test of grief.

Easter Message

Across the world there is a singing,
    Melodic voices send a cry
Of joyousness, of great rejoicing
    Across the rafters of the sky.
There is a note of triumph ringing
    That brightens every heart that hears,
And ever shall this song of gladness
    Peal out across the coming years.

The Christ is risen! O, this message
    Proclaims that victory is won.
Death could not hold Him with its coldness
    And He walked forth, God's holy Son.
And radiant hope bursts forth with gladness,
    Triumphant, joyous, filled with power.
The Christ is risen! Cease all weeping.
    There is a glory in this hour.

God Hears Our Prayers

If we will bow in silent prayer
And pray with faith, with strong belief,
Ask God to ease the load we bear
Or give us strength to bear our grief,
In infinite compassion God will take
Away our burden, ease our painful ache.

For when we speak to God of need,
His answer soon will come. His hand
Will graciously reach down and lead
Our feet to a higher, brighter land.
When we forget our anxiousness and care
And speak to God, He hears — for He is there.

Seekers

We who are hungry for the bread
That satisfies the heart and soul,
Possess a longing to be led
To where the living waters roll.

And we who need the healing balm
That heals a broken, saddened heart,
Must seek to find the inward calm
Which shall remain and not depart.

God's Edict

When hearts are filled with sorrow, words of cheer
Will lift them up. A kindly, friendly word
Of comfort, praise, or of encouragement
May be the thing, whenever it is heard,
To raise a heartsick soul
And make it whole.

Compassion is an edict of our God.
A sympathetic friendliness will make
A weak heart strong, will take away the pain,
Will overcome the sorrow and the ache.
Compassion's gentle glow
We each must know.

Solace

The passing of our loved ones brings
    Much bitter pain and grief,
But there's comfort in the knowledge
    That our loneliness is brief.

A bright and endless day awaits
    Beyond the silent night,
For death is but the door that leads
    To everlasting light.

Love's Rejuvenation

When daily burdens cower me,
    Seem more than I can bear,
A quiet little talk with God,
    A silent little prayer
Can take away my gloom and fear,
    Can drive my care away
And put a gladness in my heart
    And sunshine in my day.
Once more, I find that I can go
    To take an active part
In everyday affairs — I have
    God's peace within my heart.

Song of Release

Out of sorrow, out of pain,
    I shall make a glorious song,
    One so beautiful, so strong,
Other sufferers shall gain
From its high clear note of cheer.
    I shall sing of peace, relief
    From the tentacles of grief,
And each sufferer shall hear.

I shall sing and lift each heart.
    I shall make a song of light,
    One of radiance, so bright
It will rend the dark apart.
Every listener shall find
    All the high, clear, liquid notes
    Echoed from a thousand throats,
Will open vistas of the mind!

The Wings of Grief

O Heart, when sorrow seems too hard to bear,
Do not give way to grief, but say a prayer.

There will be joy again beyond belief;
Forget the burden brought to you by grief.

There will be sunlit roads to walk upon;
God's hand will not withhold a radiant dawn.

Sometimes vicissitudes are but the wings
That bear you on to greater, better things.

Nature of Acceptance

There are those who know great hope and gladness
If they can visualize one gleam of light
Which, breaking through their barrier of darkness,
Brings them new life and takes away their night.

And there are others who will dress in mourning,
Who weep and grieve their dismal lives away,
If just one brief hour of darkness comes,
Hopelessly they let their sorrow stay.

Tears

Surely the hand of God must spread
The peace and calm which follow grief,
No matter whose the tears are shed:
The good, the bad; the priest, the thief.

There is a beauty past believing
In tears which cleanse the heart of stain,
For in the purity of grieving
God's soothing balm relieves the pain.

60

Prayer

"Whatsoever ye shall ask in prayer, believing, ye shall receive."

Matthew 21:22

Prayer

God may be invisible to our eyes, but He is ever visible to our hearts. Especially is He visible to us when we will pray with earnestness and sincerity. If we compose ourselves and open our hearts to Him, we will find that He is very near and that He listens to us. Christianity is a religion of a living God, not a dead God, as some would have us believe.

Nothing can transform us as much as sincere prayer. When we pray, we shed our burdens; our souls become light again. We shift the responsibility to stronger shoulders, feeling joyful and confident. Our faith and trust are assured, for we know that God will not fail us. We should pray always, not only when we are in need or in affliction or are desperate for help.

Each prayer that we make should come from a believing and humble heart. We should remember to express gratitude for blessings received. Prayer should never be made from habit nor become repetitious. We should plead and not demand; we should ask and not command.

When we pray, we surrender ourselves to the influence of the Holy Spirit. In prayer, we leave our infinitesimal selves behind and put ourselves into the hands of Someone who is greater than we are. We put ourselves at God's disposal, and ask that His will, not ours, be done.

When we pray, it is God at work within our hearts. In Romans 8:26, we are told that "The Spirit also helpeth our infirmities: for we know not what we should pray for as we ought; but the Spirit itself maketh intercession for us."

Prayer is an act of faith and hope. God has promised us that faith the size of a mustard seed will remove mountains. But God does not always answer our prayers in precisely the way we may want them answered. His knowledge is much greater than ours; He is well aware of our needs. He gives us what is best for us, the things that we need, not always the things for which we have asked.

In Matthew 21:22, we read: "And all things, whatsoever ye shall ask in prayer, believing, ye shall receive."

And in Mark 11:24, we read: "Therefore, I say unto you, What things soever ye desire, when ye pray, believe that ye receive them, and ye shall have them."

Yet, in James 4:3, we read: "Ye ask, and receive not, because ye ask amiss, that ye may consume it upon your lusts."

Also, in James 5:16, we are told: "The effectual fervent prayer of a righteous man availeth much."

In Romans 8:27, we are told that the Holy Spirit understands prayer is not always expressed in words and that He understands what is in our minds and hearts. Many prayers need no words.

Prayer can be a simple act of faith. The woman spoken of in Matthew 9:21 did not pray with words, only with her thoughts, when she, in simple faith, reached out a hand to touch the hem of the garment of Jesus. But her act was a prayer, and it was answered immediately; she was healed.

"Wait on the Lord," we are commanded in Psalm 27:14. We must have the patience to place ourselves trustingly in the hands of God and to await His will. We "Wait on the Lord," because we know that He is interested in us and in our well-being.

God loves each of us, but He does not want His love to stop

with us. His will is that we should be channels through which His love may flow to others. His bounty to us is endless, but He expects that bounty to beget bounty, and that each of us be unselfish in our attitudes. We ought to develop a great and genuine feeling of gratefulness in our hearts, and know a total willingess to share our blessings with others.

It should be comforting to everyone of us to know that we can bring our needs to God in prayer. As I Peter 5:7 states, "Casting all your care upon him; for he careth for you."

I Timothy 2:1 tells us: "I exhort therefore, that, first of all, supplications, prayers, intercessions, and giving of thanks, be made for all men."

The Word of God was made flesh so that faith could be made simple for us. Prayer is worship, with our faith and trust going to God in silent supplication and thanksgiving for His loving-kindness and mercy.

Hope

Courageous ones who face each day
Impelled by some deep inner force
Which gives them strength to go their way,
Thank God for the enduring source.

Eyes cannot see nor can ears hear
The surge of this almighty power
Which we call HOPE. But it is near;
It lives within each heart, each hour.

65

Who Seeks for God

Who seeks for God,
Will find His outstretched hand,
Will find himself
Companioned through the dark.
God's loving hand
Will lead you, He will guide
Your stumbling feet;
His radiance will mark
A path for you.
His gentle voice will calm
All inner fears;
A confidence will flame
Within your heart.
And courage, valor, pride
Will fill your soul
When God calls you by name.

Disguised Blessings

I prayed for greater strength to do my will,
But God knew best — I did not have my way,
But I grew weaker still, until I learned
Humility, so that I might obey.

66

I prayed for power that I might win great praise
And adulation, to rule with iron rod,
But I was given weakness so that I
Might know and feel a greater need of God.

I asked for what I thought were fitting things
To bring enjoyment and to make me wise,
Though not a thing I prayed for was received,
Yet blessings came to me in strange disguise!

Forgiveness

If you would be forgiven
For wrongs that you have done,
Pray earnestly to God above
And to His loving Son.

Just bow your head in sorrow,
Put other things apart,
Then cleanse your mind of everything
And speak right from your heart.

For when you come contritely
Before God's pure, white throne,
His wonderful forgiveness
Will gloriously be shown.

Prayers

A prayer can be a joy for man,
    A source of energy,
A weapon in the fight for right,
    A chant of victory.

A prayer can be a song of thanks,
    A plea for love and grace;
It may be long, it may be short,
    And said in any place.

A prayer should be inspiring to
    Each man made from the sod,
For prayers are but the stepping-stones
    Upon the path to God.

Consolation for the Heart

Somewhere there is a heart that aches,
Somewhere there is someone in pain,
But He who rules the universe
Shall see that joy will come again,
For it is certain Someone cares
And it is certain Someone knows
About our joys and happiness,
About our griefs and cares and woes.

If we but place our trust in Him
And put our burdens on His breast,
We soon shall know the peacefulness
And quietness that comes with rest.
Our worried hearts shall soon be calmed,
Our minds completely filled with ease;
Our God and Father understands;
He knows and feels, He hears and sees.

When We Pray

The act of praying
Is so satisfying;
It fills a need
Within the mind and heart.
The utterance
Of love and strong belief
Will quickly cause
All evil to depart.

The act of praying
Is a simple thing;
It is not difficult
Nor hard nor odd.
It is a reaching out
A seeking hand
To find the warm and loving
Hand of God.

Testaments of Faith

A prayer of praise that's said with words
    Can be a shining thing,
For any talk with God is good,
    Can cause the heart to sing.

But actions, too, can be a prayer
    Of praise, of hope, of cheer.
Faith can be shown in many ways
    To drive away all fear.

Vital Thing

Each one must learn this vital thing;
    Our God will answer prayer,
If prayer is made with faith and hope,
    Not words spent on the air.

All vain petitions will but die,
    For these will never rise
Within the hearing of God's throne,
    So far beyond the skies.

But earnest cries and sincere pleas
    From a believing soul
Never will be cast aside
    But always reach their goal.

70

Thanksgiving

"O give thanks unto the Lord."

Psalm 107:1

Thanksgiving

"O give thanks unto the Lord; for he is good; for his mercy endureth forever." I Chronicles 16:34.

Thankfulness of heart is one of the greatest of all principles, not only as recognition of past benefits received from God's bountiful heart, but as the activator of blessings yet to come. Thankfulness stimulates a continuous flow of blessings.

"In every thing give thanks: for this is the will of God in Christ Jesus concerning you." I Thessalonians 5:18.

"Offer unto God thanksgiving; and pay thou vows unto the most High." Psalm 50:14.

When we affirm goodness, goodness will be ours. When we affirm and declare our love, love will be given to us in return. And when we have thankfulness in our heart for our blessings, blessings will continue to be bestowed upon us by our gracious and loving heavenly Father. God gives infinitely and impartially to all His children.

It would be rare indeed if we did not, at one time or another, feel frustrated or dismayed. Each of us is human, and these things are human qualities. But it is always a comfort to know that we may turn to the Bible for reassurance. The many promises that God has made to us and the innumerable times that we can find proof of His love for us, are found there.

In Isaiah 41:10, we read: "Fear thou not; for I am with thee: be not dismayed; for I am thy God; I will strengthen thee; yea, I will help thee; yea, I will uphold thee with the right hand of my righteousness."

We must commune with God; we must strive for that reassurance of His blessed nearness to us, confident that His all-embracing love surrounds us and protects us. God is never far from us, if we will only call on His blessed name. We are never truly alone, unless we deliberately turn away from Him and put Him from us. His spiritual rewards will be given only to His faithful ones.

"Let every thing that hath breath praise the Lord. Praise ye the Lord," we are told in Psalm 150:6.

Gratitude is a song of the soul which is sung in the presence of the goodness of God. It has been termed "the memory of the heart." Our gratitude must be expressed to "the giver of every good and perfect gift." A grateful heart is often one that can find blessings in the things that so many will overlook.

Thankfulness

God put a gladness in my heart,
A radiant joy within my soul;
He heard my cry when in distress,
He set me free and made me whole.

I come now, God, to worship Thee.
Hear Thou my prayer and song of praise.
Be Thou my sword and shield. In Thee,
I put my trust through all my days.

Bread

How precious is this life-sustaining force.
How fine its sweetness. This essential food,
This manna, is God's greatest gift to man.
An elemental thing, He found it good.

Symbol of life! Touch bread with reverent hands.
Taste bread with thankfulness, and let your heart
Know full appreciation of this gift
And never let your gratefulness depart.

Shared bread is sweet. Each bit of golden crust,
Each tiny piece of soft, life-giving bread,
Is meant for nourishment. Each particle
Was meant to see that every man be fed.

Penitent

I give my all without reserve,
And I shall give my best.
I only ask that I may serve
In ways which He knows best.

I will accept the lowest place
And do what others scorn;
I only ask to see His face
And smile on that great Morn.

75

Speechless

How can I find the shining word,
    The glowing phrase
Or the triumphant chord or note,
    To tell God's praise?

The new enrichment of my heart,
    The death of doubt,
The birth of faith and hope and love,
    Must all come out

Or else I fear my heart will burst!
    How can I choose
The word, the phrase, the chord, the note
    Which I should use?

Everlasting Miracle

Christ saw the hungry multitudes
And knew compassion for their need.
"Give ye them to eat," He said,
And wrought a miracle to feed
The hungry crowd. Five little loaves
And two small fishes played a part.
This act shall live eternally
In every faithful Christian's heart.

76

A Friendly Word

A friendly word can free a man
From a tight shell and make him tall.
A friendly word can help to span
The view that keeps him mean and small.

A friendly word can cleanse the heart
And banish doubt and conquer fear.
To one who walks a space apart,
A friendly word can draw him near.

Thankfulness for Little Things

A whole, sweet loaf was never mine.
    I gather avidly
The tiny morsels, kernel bits,
    Which are for me.

But I am thankful for these crumbs,
    Crumbs without wine —
There have been days I had not these
    To claim as mine!

Make Men Aware!

Until men know His Spirit,
    None will find
A grateful heart or know
    A peaceful mind.

Tell of His glory; speak
    Of sacrifice;
Make all the world aware
    Of Lord and Christ!

Good Harvest

Though new-turned earth went back to crust,
Then changed to mire by cold, bleak rain;
Though leaf was tinged with rot and rust
And stem was twisted as with pain;
Despite these elemental things,
The vernal blades that burst from ground
Seemed touched by God's own angels' wings;
The kernel of the wheat was sound!

Peace

"My peace I give unto you."

John 14:27

Peace

"Blessed are the peacemakers: for they shall be called the children of God." Matthew 5:9.

Peace is the divinely intended relationship between man and man and between man and God. This means individually as well as collectively. Peace represents our ideals of justice, freedom, dignity, brotherhood, as well a fraternity of the spirit.

Peace was the central theme in the life of Jesus. He did not love peace only in principle, but rather loved the people and knew that they needed peace in their hearts to realize God's will for their lives. Jesus offered a new life to those who would follow Him, a new life of purity, trust, love, and faith. He bridged the wide chasm between the Jew and the Gentile and between the Jew and the Samaritan.

The peace of God passeth all understanding.

Our only hope for peace begins with the renewal of belief in and loyalty to God as the author and guarantor of peace. "Create in me a clean heart, O God; and renew a right spirit within me," sings the Psalmist in Psalm 51:10.

Our hope for peace begins with an humble adoration to the One in whose will for peace we find our peace. "Peace I leave with you, my peace I give unto you." John 14:27.

The peace spoken of by Jesus Christ our Lord and Saviour was not of this earth. Peace is a settling influence, removing anxiety and fear and doubt and bestowing courage and strength and confidence.

Jesus Christ was the personification of God's Word of

81

Peace. We are told in Jeremiah 29:11: "For I know the thoughts that I think toward you, saith the Lord, thoughts of peace and not of evil."

"Therefore, being justified by faith, we have peace with God through our Lord Jesus Christ." Romans 5:1.

In the temple, in Jerusalem, the devout Simeon held in his arms the infant Jesus, the living expression of God's thoughts of peace. And, like Simeon, we can face our departure from this life with confidence and in peace if we are the possessors of the peace that passes all understanding.

Harmonious Being

There is a goodness in the heart of man,
A consciousness of love and brotherhood,
A radiance of life that is a plan
Of One whose life was perfect, whole and good.

This is the Life of God that is within me.
It shall remove all doubt and every fear.
I have a wholeness which is plain to see;
I am but an extension of His sphere.

I see God everywhere. In unity
Of mind and spirit, body, soul and heart,
His law is written. This shall always be,
For perfect harmony shall not depart.

Prayer for Quietness

Ease the pounding of my heartbeat
And the torture of my brain,
Lift the burden of my spirit,
Give me peacefulness again.

Break the tensions which enfold me,
Help me feel the blessed power
Which will come when hurt has lessened
And I know a quieting hour.

Still the tumult and the shouting,
Let the mad confusion cease;
Let Thy radiance and glory
Bring me everlasting peace.

Consolation

Out of a wild, dark sky
    Comes peaceful rain
And out of deepest grief
    Comes healing pain.

Out of a fight for right
    Comes victory
And out of a patient heart,
    Tranquillity.

83

Miracles

Our God can take a bit of earth
    And warm it with His sun
And give it drink with His soft rain
    And then, when this is done,
Implant a tiny seed within
    The heart of the damp earth,
And soon produce a miracle—
    The miracle of birth.

Our God can take an evil soul,
    A wicked, sin-filled heart,
And purify them, make them clean,
    Give them a fresh, new start;
And if the heart accepts with faith
    The Holy Spirit's will
And trusts in Him, there will appear
    Another miracle.

Heart's Radiant Hour

How can a heart not see the light?
    How can it fail to know
Some pathways lead to wrong, not right,
    And these it should not go?

But hearts are blind when ruled by sin,
    For great is sin's dark power.
But when God's love can shine within,
    Heart knows a radiant hour.

Man's Hour of Peace

Man's hour of peace
Is something man must earn,
It is not given him.
A man must learn
The rest he gains from hours
Of care and strife
Is payment earned,
But needed in his life.

A man who wins
Contentment for his soul
Must battle for it
As he would a goal.
The idler and the shirker
Never can
Experience the reward
Of working man.

Heart and Spirit

When spirit lags, becomes inert,
When heart is faint and filled with fear
And knows a deep and conscious hurt,
Then living seems so bleak and drear.

But when, exuberant and gay,
The heart grows jubilant and strong,
The hurt, dejected, goes away
And soul and spirit sing a song.

Benefactor

The Lord provides an inner peace,
Serenity and restfulness;
To those who call upon His name,
He gives His grace and blessedness.

Though disappointments may provoke
And aggravations try your soul,
Hearts may step lightly over these
If eyes are on a farther goal.

Worldly follies may mislead you
And sorrow may beset your heart,
Still Christ the Lord will be with you
And where He is, these things depart.

With Peaceful Heart

Man longs for peacefulness again
When heart is sore and spirit tried
By thorns of multitudes and throngs,
By being hemmed in on each side.

When hurricanes within his being
Are caused by things which would oppress,
Man needs tranquillity and peace,
To find his God in quietness.

Quietness

The heart is hurt with hurriedness and flurry,
With agonizing trouble, fear, and care;
Through spendthrift haste and wild futility,
The heart has often more than it can bear.

"In quietness shall be your strength." These words
The heart should ponder and all clamor cease,
For only blessed quietness shall bring
A soothing relaxation, healing peace.

Sharing

Some give and never
Feel the loss
For they have plenty
For tomorow.
But this is not
True charity,
And they may know
Regret and sorrow.

A gift from large
And full supply
Is really not
A gift at all.
But only he
Who shares his loaf
Can walk light-hearted,
Proud and tall.